PASSOVER

Angela Wood

WAYLAND

CARNIVAL

CHINESE NEW YEAR

CHRISTMAS

DIWALI

ID-UL-FITR

Editor: Penny McDowell
Series editor: Sarah Doughty
Series designer: Tim Mayer
Book designer: Malcolm Walker

First published in 1997 by Wayland Publishers Ltd
61 Western Road, Hove, East Sussex, BN3 1JD

British Library Cataloguing in Publication Data
Wood, Angela
  Passover. – (Festivals)
  1. Passover – Juvenile literature
  I. Title
  394.2′68′296

ISBN 0 7502 1941 6

Printed and bound by L.E.G.O. S.p.A., Vicenza, Italy

A note on pronunciation
In Hebrew, there is a throaty sound which sounds like the 'ch' in 'loch' or 'Bach'. In some books, it is written with the letters 'ch' but it does not sound like the 'ch' in 'chips'. In this book and some others, it is written as 'h', for example, Pesah and hametz.

For Uncle Sam,
my American uncle,
and his family
because they
treasure freedom

Picture acknowledgements
Commissioned photography by Guy Hall 12 (top), 22, 23 (both), 25 (bottom) and Rupert Horrox title page, 5, 17, 18, 19, 20, 21, 24, 26; Photri cover (centre), 7; Zev Radovan 11 (bottom), 12 (bottom), 13, 15 (both), 17 (bottom), 25 (top), 27, 28; Trip 10 (Helen Rogers), 16 (bottom) (E James); Angela Wood 8, 9, 11 (top), 14 (both), 29 (both); Zefa cover (top, bottom and bottom left), 16 (top).

The photograph on page 10 is by Mr Heinz Seelig, published by Palphot, Herzlia, Israel.
The photograph on page 21 was published in 'Diaspora Haggadah' by Yanin Enterprises, Israel in 1988.

The author would especially like to thank Ester Gluck, the Greenbury family, Rabbi Hugo Gryn and Rabbi Willi Wolff. Also, Neil and Sandra Pike and their children.

A note on dates
Each religion has its own system for counting the years of its history. The starting point may be related to the birth or death of a special person or an important event. In everyday life, today, when different communities have dealings with each other, they need to use the same counting system for setting dates in the future and writing accounts of the past. The Western system is now used throughout the world. It is based on Christian beliefs about Jesus: AD (Anno Domini = in the year of our Lord) and BC (Before Christ). Members of the various world faiths use the common Western system, but, instead of AD and BC, they say and write CE (in the Common Era) and BCE (before the Common Era).

CONTENTS

JEWS AROUND THE WORLD

These countries especially helped Jews during the Holocaust.

For hundreds of years, until the twentieth century, most Jews lived in this part of Europe. When the Nazis occupied it in the 1930s and 1940s, Jews fled if they could. Almost all those who stayed were murdered by the Nazis.

SCANDINAVIA

EASTERN EUROPE

RUSSIA (FORMER SOVIET UNION)

Jews have lived here for about 1,500 years. They were treated very badly, especially in the late nineteenth and early twentieth century. Many emigrated to the land of Israel and to the USA. They were not recognized in the Soviet Union and many wished to leave but were refused permission. They called themselves 'refuseniks'. It is now easier for them to leave and many live in Israel.

PORTUGAL

SPAIN

Jews lived peacefully under Muslim rule but were treated very badly under Roman Catholic rule. In the 1490s, the Jews were driven out of Spain and Portugal.

NORTH AFRICA

Jews lived in these areas for over 2,000 years but many left for Israel after 1948.

ISRAEL

Once known as Babylonia, Jews were taken into exile here in 586 BCE when Jerusalem, the capital, was attacked and the first temple was destroyed. Seventy years later they were able to return but most had settled there and stayed. A second temple was built in Jerusalem.

IRAN

CHINA

INDIA

There have been Jews in India for over 2,000 years. They call themselves 'the children of Israel'. Since 1948, almost all have left to live in Israel or English-speaking countries.

ETHIOPIA

There have probably been Jews in Ethiopia for almost 3,000 years. They call themselves 'the house of Israel'. They were treated very badly, especially in the 1980s, and many fled to Israel or were rescued by Israelis.

SOUTH AFRICA

Small numbers of Jews escaped the Holocaust and settled here.

The Jewish people settled in the land of Israel over 3,000 years ago and believe that God gave it to them. It was occupied many times by foreign powers. The Romans destroyed the second temple in 70 CE and Jews dispersed to surrounding areas. Jews really began returning to Israel at the end of the nineteenth century. Israel is the homeland for Jews all over the world and over a third of Jews in the world live there now. It became a modern state in 1948.

AUSTRALIA

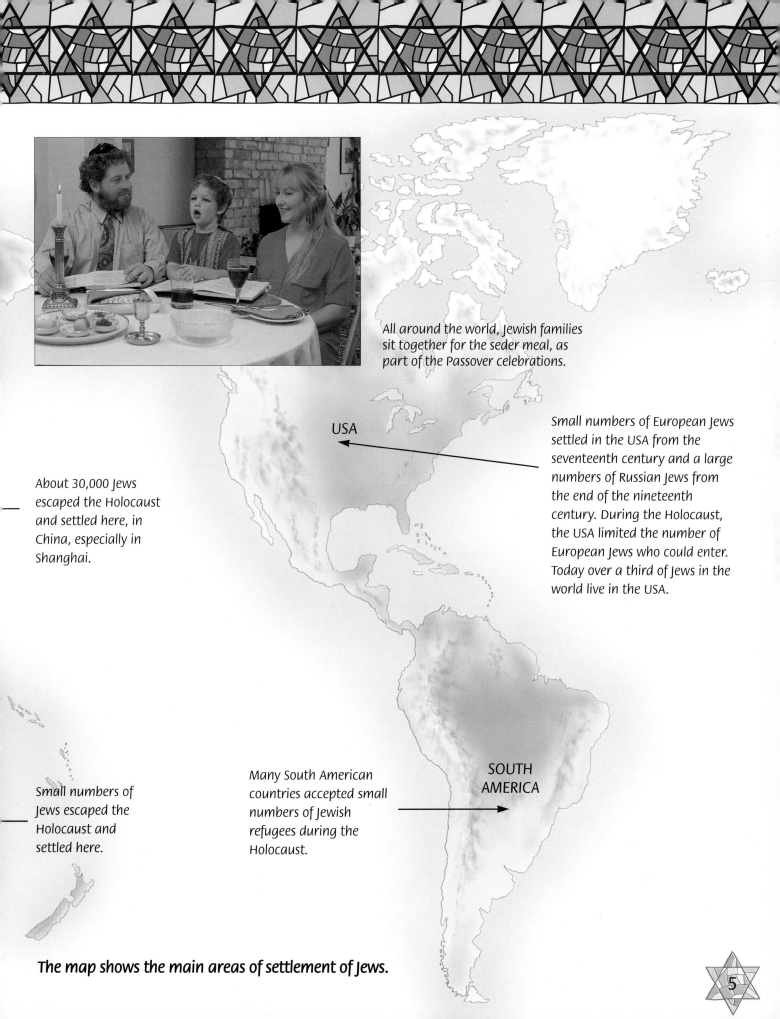

All around the world, Jewish families sit together for the seder meal, as part of the Passover celebrations.

USA

Small numbers of European Jews settled in the USA from the seventeenth century and a large numbers of Russian Jews from the end of the nineteenth century. During the Holocaust, the USA limited the number of European Jews who could enter. Today over a third of Jews in the world live in the USA.

About 30,000 Jews escaped the Holocaust and settled here, in China, especially in Shanghai.

Small numbers of Jews escaped the Holocaust and settled here.

Many South American countries accepted small numbers of Jewish refugees during the Holocaust.

SOUTH AMERICA

The map shows the main areas of settlement of Jews.

WE WANT TO BE FREE

Passover is a Jewish festival based on events that took place about 3,000 years ago. It is one of the most important festivals in the Jewish calendar. Passover lasts for over a week and is celebrated in March or April each year.

In English, the festival is known as Passover because long, long ago at a very difficult time of suffering for the Jews, death passed over their homes and they were spared. The main Hebrew name for the festival, Pesa<u>h</u> (or Pesach), has the same meaning.

PASSOVER NAMES

Jews also use these Hebrew names:

<u>H</u>ag ha'aviv (which means spring festival) because it falls in springtime in the land of Israel, which is the Jewish people's homeland.

<u>H</u>ag ha'matzot (which means festival of unleavened bread) because matzot (plural) (unleavened bread) are eaten during the festival instead of ordinary bread.

Z'man herutenu (which means season of our freedom) because it is a time when Jews remember and relive their escape from slavery.

The most important theme of Passover is freedom, and the festival shows us how much Jewish people value freedom for themselves and all people. The heart of the festival is the story of how the Jews' ancestors, who were slaves, had a miraculous escape to freedom. The story is told every year in a dramatic and lively way.

The heart of Pesa<u>h</u> is the seder, a special meal eaten on the first evening, to celebrate freedom. It is celebrated in very similar ways all over the world but each family and culture has its own special customs. This is a Jewish family, from Yemen.

LET MY PEOPLE GO!

Over 3,000 years ago, the ancient Jews (called Hebrews or Israelites) lived in Egypt, which was ruled by pharaohs. At first, life was good, but then a cruel pharaoh took over. He made them into slaves and ordered them to build many new buildings. They worked hard and long each day, with no rest and hardly any food or water.

This picture is from a haggadah printed in the USA in 1949. It shows the kind of work that the slaves in Egypt had to do, the harsh way they were treated and how they suffered.

The pharaoh ordered that all Hebrew baby boys should be killed but the Hebrew midwives refused to do this. One Hebrew woman, Yoheved, hid her baby boy by the river in a watertight basket so that he would not be killed. The pharaoh's daughter found him and took him to her father's palace. The baby was called Moshe (Moses, in English) and grew up as an Egyptian prince. Even so, he knew that he was really a Hebrew.

One day, Moshe saw an Egyptian beating a slave. Moshe was so angry that he killed the slave driver. He realized that he might be caught and punished for killing an Egyptian, so he ran away into the wilderness.

Moshe lived there for some years. He worked for a shepherd and married the shepherd's daughter, Zipporah. One day, Moshe heard God tell him to return to Egypt to free the slaves. God spoke to him out of a burning bush whose flames did not go out. God told him to meet the pharaoh and say to him, 'Let my people go'. God said that Moshe's brother, Aaron, would help him. God promised to be with him, too.

This painting by Philip Ratner shows Moshe at the burning bush. When Moshe heard God speaking to him, he felt strange and frightened. He wanted to know God's name and heard God saying, 'I am what I am.'

9

A MIRACULOUS ESCAPE

Moshe went back to Egypt to plead with the pharaoh to free his people, but the pharaoh refused. Soon after, the Egyptians, but not the Hebrews, suffered ten plagues. The pharaoh did not change his mind until the tenth plague which began to kill Egyptian babies. At last, he let the slaves go.

This is a page of a modern haggadah from Israel showing the ten plagues. Hebrew is read from right to left and these pictures run from right to left starting at the top.

THE TEN PLAGUES

The river turning to blood
Thousands of frogs
People getting lice
Wild beasts roaming the land
Cattle becoming diseased
People getting nasty boils
Large hailstones falling
Locusts swarming everywhere
Darkness in the daytime
First-born Egyptian babies dying.

Moshe told his people to get ready to leave that night. The Hebrews were afraid, but excited. Each family had already made bread dough and left it in a warm place to rise so that they could bake it in the morning. But that night there was no time to wait for the dough to rise so they baked it as it was and it came out flat. They took it for food on their journey.

A week later they reached a stretch of water called the Sea of Reeds (or the Red Sea). In the meantime, the pharaoh changed his mind and sent soldiers after the Hebrews. Moshe led his people across on dry land through the sea. The soldiers tried to follow, but the waters rose and covered them and they never made it. When the slaves were safe on the other side, Miriam, Moshe's sister, and some other women started to dance and sing.

The Hebrews believed that they were only able to escape because God made it happen. It is the most important experience in Jewish history and has helped the Jewish people to value freedom and feel for other people who are slaves or strangers.

Above: This painting by Philip Ratner shows the crossing of the Sea of Reeds. It is hard to imagine, but the Bible says that when Moshe stretched out his arm, God made the waters part.

This fourteenth-century Spanish haggadah shows Moshe's sister Miriam and other women leading the singing and dancing with tambourines to celebrate the crossing of the Sea of Reeds.

WHAT TO EAT?

Food is a very important part of the celebration of Pesah (Passover). Like their ancestors who took unleavened bread on their journey, Jews do not eat leavened bread at all during Pesah. Instead of ordinary bread, they eat unleavened bread called matzah. Jewish shops and some supermarkets sell matzah and other Pesah food.

It is surprising how many ordinary foods contain hametz. The food in this shop window is all hametz-free. Jews who wish to follow Pesah strictly, buy foods like this for the festival.

Foods that contain leaven are called hametz. Hametz is the fermented grain of wheat, oats, barley, rye or spelt. Hametz can also be anything that is used to make food leaven, such as yeast or baking powder.

Today, matzah is made in Jewish bakeries and food factories. The bakers are very careful not to let any hametz get into the matzah at any time.

These young people are rolling out matzah dough. The stainless steel work surface has been washed since the last batch of dough because any dough left on it would start to rise and spoil the next batch.

This man is baking matzah in the traditional way by putting the dough in the oven on wooden poles. When the matzah is cooked, it is still slightly soft, but it crisps up as it cools.

So that the dough does not rise on its own, the bakers have only 18 minutes to make and bake matzah. To beat the clock, they usually work as a team. After washing their hands, they have to: set the clock... measure the flour and water... pour the water into the flour... mix them together... knead the dough... roll it out flat... cut it into the right size pieces... and put it in a hot oven to bake.

ASHKENAZI AND SEPHARDI JEWS

In the Jewish world, there are two main cultural groups: Ashkenazi Jews who mostly originated in northern Europe and North America, and Sephardi Jews who originated in southern Europe and the Middle East. There are some differences between Sephardi and Ashkenazi Jews in the way they live. Ashkenazi Jews regard certain other foods as <u>h</u>ametz and do not eat them during Pesa<u>h</u> (for example, peas, corn, beans and rice). Whereas Sephardi Jews do eat these foods and actually eat quite a lot of rice dishes.

COUNTDOWN TO PESA<u>H</u>

The weeks leading up to Pesa<u>h</u> are the busiest time in the whole year and some families start spring-cleaning vigorously about a month beforehand. Not only is it important not to eat <u>h</u>ametz during Pesa<u>h</u>, but Jews must also make sure that they do not have any around the house. Jews who work with <u>h</u>ametz, for example bakers or grocers, sell the <u>h</u>ametz before Pesa<u>h</u> and then buy it back afterwards.

Families clean their homes from top to bottom to make it free of <u>h</u>ametz. The kitchen is the most important area to be cleaned, but it is usually left until last so that the family can go on eating normally during all the preparations. Many families have special serving dishes which are only used for Pesa<u>h</u>.

On the morning before Pesa<u>h</u>, Jews burn the remains of all the food they will not eat during Pesa<u>h</u>. This little girl is helping to tend the fire in her garden.

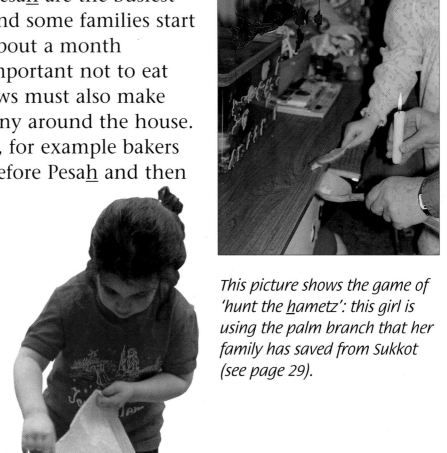

This picture shows the game of 'hunt the <u>h</u>ametz': this girl is using the palm branch that her family has saved from Sukkot (see page 29).

By the evening before Pesah, the house is almost completely clear of hametz. As part of the festival, families search for hametz to make sure that there is none left in the house. Usually one of the adults hides small pieces of hametz and the children have to hunt for them. They turn down the lights, take a candle, a feather and a little paper bag or some other container and start looking in every corner. When they find a piece of hametz, they scoop it into the bag with the feather. Then they take the bag of hametz outside. The next morning, they burn the hametz and say, 'May all the hametz that we have, whether we have seen it or not, whether we have removed it or not, be counted as nothing, like dust.'

Not everyone has a place outside where they can burn hametz. In Jerusalem, Israel, communities burn their hametz together on waste ground.

Some families use ordinary dishes at Pesah. They make metal items usable by dipping them completely in boiling water. In Jerusalem, there are large vats where people can take their cutlery and pots to be boiled.

SEDER COUNTDOWN

The seder is a special supper which is held on the first evening of Pesa<u>h</u>. It is the highlight of the festival in Jewish homes all over the world. A seder usually lasts for three to six hours. It is not just a meal, but also includes singing, discussion, storytelling, rituals and the tasting of symbolic foods. Everybody around the table takes part and the children are particularly encouraged to join in.

Before the seder begins, the grandmother or mother lights candles to bring light and joy to the occasion. The seder is arranged in two parts, with a full meal in the middle. The word seder means order, because each stage of the celebration follows a certain order. The meal and the two parts are made up of fourteen steps:

In some Jewish families and communities, the leader of the seder wears a white gown. This family lives in Israel, but follows some of the Persian Sephardi customs because the family is from Iran (Persia).

1. Kiddush
Jews say or sing blessings for the festival.

2. Washing the hands
The leader of the seder washes their hands, so that they will be clean for handing round the symbolic foods.

Usually a man leads the seder. He washes his hands twice – the first time before handing out the karpas and the second time before handing out the matzah for people to eat. However, at some seders everybody washes their hands.

3. Karpas

This is a vegetable and everybody gets a piece, dipped in saltwater or vinegar (see pages 22–23).

4. Dividing the matzah

There are three matzot (plural) in layers of cloth. The middle matzah is broken and half is put back. An adult hides the other half, called the afikomen.

5. Telling the story

This is the longest section of the seder and has many songs and poems.

6. Washing the hands

This time, the leader of the seder says a blessing for hand washing because there will be matzah to eat and the meal will come soon.

7. Blessings for matzah

There is a blessing for bread, because matzah is a kind of bread and then a blessing for the matzah itself. Then the leader of the seder breaks the matzah and everyone gets a piece to eat – the first piece on Pesa<u>h</u>!

The leader of the seder breaks a piece of matzah in two, puts one piece back under the matzah cover and hides the other piece for the children to find later. He lifts the matzah cover and says, 'Let all who are hungry come and eat . . .'

This is the table of an Ashkenazi seder. The matzot have been made by hand and that is why they are uneven. Next to the partly covered matzot is an open haggadah.

17

8. The bitter vegetable

Everybody eats a piece of a bitter vegetable to remind them of slavery (see pages 22–23).

9. Sandwich

A piece of maror (a bitter vegetable) is eaten between two pieces of matzah so that the two important tastes and feelings are brought together.

10. The meal

Families may have any Pesah food to eat. The meal is not rushed. Towards the end of the meal – usually while the adults relax and chat – the children set off to hunt for the afikomen. In most families, the children get a prize for finding the afikomen.

Ashkenazi Jews often use a piece of horseradish for the bitter vegetable. This is a piece of maror eaten between two pieces of matzah. Sephardi Jews often use the inside stalk of a lettuce. Whatever is used, it always tastes horrible!

11. The hidden matzah

When the afikomen is brought back and shared, it joins the past and the future together because it came from the first part of the seder and the second part is now beginning.

Some of these children are looking for the afikomen everywhere they can think of, while one child has already found it!

12. Thanksgiving for the meal

This is a series of verses and songs, to say thank you to God for the food.

13. Praise

Songs of praise for freedom are sung and thoughts turn to the future of the world.

14. Conclusion

THE FOUR CUPS, QUESTIONS AND CHILDREN

At four points in the seder, everyone drinks a glass of wine or grape juice. It is said that drinking four times reflects and celebrates the four ways that God helped the Hebrews to become free. This comes from the special Jewish book, the Torah: 'I will bring you out; I will deliver you; I will redeem you; I will take you to me.'

Early on in the seder, in the 'telling the story' step, a child (or children) sings four questions. The questions ask why the seder night is different from any other time of the year. The adults encourage children to ask their own questions at any time during the seder.

Singing the four questions is sometimes a nervous moment for the youngest child, but a proud moment for the parents.

SONG

Why is this night unlike other nights?

For we may not eat bread
but matzah instead
yes matzah instead.
For tonight is the night,
we eat matzah for our bread.

For we eat bitter things
to remember the stings
and the pain of slavery.
For tonight is the night,
we thank God who set us free.

For we dip in the tears
that we shed through the years
the herbs that we eat.
For tonight is the night,
we think about their tears.

For on this special night,
we do not sit upright
but lean in luxury.
For tonight is the night,
we remember we are free.

This is a picture of the four children taken from a modern haggadah. The wise child is reading thoughtfully; the naughty child is selfish and stamping on a small animal; the simple child is singing in a tree and the child who does not know how to ask questions is doing handstands.

Soon after this song, there is a story about four different kinds of children, which shows adults that they should see children as individuals and teach them in the way that each child can best understand.

'DIPPING' AND 'FLICKING'

One verse of the four questions song mentions dipping herbs. There are two 'dipping' actions in the seder.

The first is the dipping of karpas in saltwater during the 'telling the story' step. Some families use cooked potato for karpas. Other families use a green vegetable. This is because green reminds them of spring – the season when the ancient Hebrews escaped from slavery. The karpas is dipped in saltwater before it is eaten because of the salty tears and sweat of the slaves. It helps Jews to feel like slaves, so that they can feel for slaves.

For karpas, this girl is about to eat a sprig of parsley, already dipped in saltwater.

The second dipping comes in 'the bitter vegetable' step. The bitter vegetable is called maror and it represents the harshness and bitterness of slavery. The maror is eaten with some haroset, a mixture that looks like the mortar which the slaves used in building. But the haroset tastes sweet because the story has a happy ending.

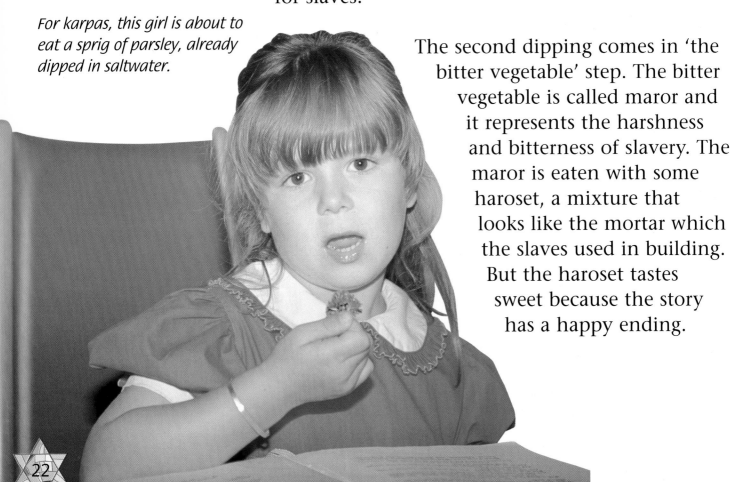

Between the two 'dippings', there is a 'flicking' while the ten plagues are read out. As each one is mentioned, everyone dips a finger into their glass of wine or grape juice and flicks it on to a cloth or plate. It is as if they are wasting some of their joy on purpose as they remember that Egyptians suffered the ten plagues before the Hebrews were set free.

This girl has dipped her fingers in wine and is flicking it to 'waste' some of her joy. When Jews remember their freedom, they also remember the suffering of the Egyptians and because of this, they cannot feel completely happy.

In the 'sandwich' step, everyone takes a piece of maror and puts it between two small pieces of matzah and eats it.

This man is dipping a piece of matzah in haroset which looks like the mortar that the Hebrew slaves used for building. But this mixture tastes sweet! Ashkenazi Jews often make haroset with grated apples, nuts and honey. Sephardi Jews often use dates and nuts.

WATCHING AND WAITING

Elijah is an important figure from Jewish history who lived almost 3,000 years ago. He was a prophet in the land of Israel. One day Elijah was carried up to heaven in a fiery chariot and no one saw him die or ever found his body. So a Jewish legend grew up that Elijah may somehow still be alive and that he appears whenever he is needed, and then disappears again. It is also thought that one day he will return with the good news that the Messiah is on the way.

Some families open the door of the room for Elijah, but others, like this one, open their front door and look both ways to see if he is coming down the street.

When the table is set for the seder, an empty cup known as 'Elijah's Cup', is placed in the middle of the table. During the second part of the seder, someone fills 'Elijah's Cup' with wine right to the top. Someone else goes to open the door for Elijah, as if to welcome him and let him in, and hear the news that the days of the Messiah will arrive soon. Children love to watch the level of wine in 'Elijah's Cup' to see if it has gone down.

Right at the end of the seder, there is a song that says that the seder is over. The seder ends with a song of hope that the Jewish people will be happy and free in their own land.

Sleepy children are carried to their beds, but many grown-ups stay up late into the night, talking and singing either traditional or modern songs about freedom.

Elijah's cup has a special place in the centre of the seder table. Many families use a special cup for Elijah because, if he comes, he will be a very special guest.

It has been a busy day and an exciting evening. Near the end of the seder, the children are often so tired that they fall asleep at the table and sometimes underneath it!

A HOLIDAY WEEK

The days at the beginning and end of Pesah are days of rest and worship. In orthodox families outside Israel, these are the first and second, and the seventh and eighth days of Pesah. In Israel and non-orthodox communities around the world, these are the first and seventh days. On these days, there are services in synagogues, with special readings from the Torah about Pesah. These include the stories about the escape from slavery.

On the middle days of Pesah people go to work if they have to, but try not to work more than is necessary. Jewish schools throughout the world are on holiday. In Israel, quite a lot of people take their annual holiday during Pesah. The weather is warm and it is a good time for family outings. Some groups organize hikes and treasure hunts in the countryside.

צְרוֹר הַמֹּר דּוֹדִי לִי בֵּין שָׁדַי יָלִין: אֶשְׁכֹּל הַכֹּפֶר
דּוֹדִי לִי בְּכַרְמֵי עֵין גֶּדִי: הִנָּךְ יָפָה רַעְיָתִי הִנָּךְ
יָפָה עֵינַיִךְ יוֹנִים: הִנְּךָ יָפֶה דוֹדִי אַף נָעִים אַף
עַרְשֵׂנוּ רַעֲנָנָה: קֹרוֹת בָּתֵּינוּ אֲרָזִים רַהִיטֵנוּ בְּרוֹתִים:

This image is from a book of the Song of Songs, made in Jerusalem in 1923. It illustrates the lines: 'You are beautiful, my love. Your eyes are like doves . . . The beams of our house are cedars and our rafters are firs.'

One of the special readings for Pesa<u>h</u> is part of the 'Song of Songs' which is in the Bible. It is a poem about love between a man and a woman and it is also understood as a poem about love between God and the Jewish people. It fits in with Pesa<u>h</u> as this is a time when Jews realize God's love for them, which was first felt when they were set free.

Many Jews who live in or come from North Africa and the Middle East have a local festival on the day after Pesa<u>h</u>. It is called maimuna. Families go on picnics and there are often fairs, street parties and outdoor concerts or shows.

This maimuna fair is being enjoyed by thousands of people. There are barbecues for food and games to play.

THE JEWISH CALENDAR

The annual festivals given in the Torah fall into two groups:

High holy days

Rosh Hashanah (New Year) and **Yom Kippur** (Day of Atonement) September or early October.
A time for saying sorry and asking forgiveness from others and making a fresh start for the new year. On Rosh Hashanah, a *shofar* (ram's horn) is blown for 'awakening' and calling all Jews to repent. It is a custom to eat pieces of apple dipped in honey for a sweet new year. Yom Kippur is a day of confession. Jews fast for 25 hours, from sunset to sunset.

The shofar *is blown in the period leading up to Rosh Hashanah and on Rosh Hashanah morning. It is also blown at the end of Yom Kippur to announce that the fast is over.*

Pilgrim festivals

These include Pesa<u>h</u>, as well as Shavuot (Festival of Weeks) and Sukkot (Festival of Booths).

Shavuot May or June.
It celebrates the giving of the Torah to Moshe while the ancient Jews were in the wilderness. It is celebrated by decorating homes and synagogues with flowers, by staying up all night to read, study and discuss the Torah, and by eating dairy foods, such as cheesecake, cheese or creamy pancakes and ice-cream.

Sukkot September or October.
Occurs five days after Yom Kippur. It celebrates the time when the ancient Jews wandered for forty

As the Torah is paraded, children join in, waving flags and singing. After the Torah is read, the adults often throw handfuls of sweets for the children to catch. This shows the idea of the Torah as sweetness.

years before they reached their homeland, Israel. They had to live in huts and today Jews build temporary homes outdoors and live in them for eight days. At the end of Sukkot comes Sim<u>h</u>at Torah (Rejoicing in Torah). The Torah scrolls are paraded in the synagogue to celebrate finishing the reading of the whole Torah which has taken a year. Then a few verses are read from the end, followed by a few verses from the beginning.
This shows that the Torah goes on for ever.

There is very little time after Yom Kippur to build the sukkah and everyone lends a hand hammering nails, tying leaves and hanging fruit.

GLOSSARY

Atonement Feeling in harmony with, and close to, God.

Confession Telling God or another person about something that you have done wrong and are sorry about.

Fermented Broken down substances in food and liquids, especially when warm. When dough is fermented, it expands and rises.

Haggadah The book used for telling the story of Pesah. The word means 'telling a story'. It is written and read in Hebrew, but is also translated into many languages so that everyone can understand.

Kiddush 'Holiness'; a song of blessings for Pesa<u>h</u>, sung at the beginning of the seder, with wine or grape juice.

Knead To push and pull dough with knuckles and hands to mix it well and get air into it.

Mortar A mixture of lime with cement, or sand and water that is used to stick bricks together in building.

Orthodox Orthodox Jews strictly follow the rituals and traditions of the Jewish religion.

Pharaoh The name given to the rulers of ancient Egypt.

Plague A deadly disease that spreads rapidly over a wide area.

Prophet A person who teaches and explains the word of God and tells people how God wants them to behave.

Repent Feel sorry about something wrong you have done and try to make that right again.

Rituals Actions, especially in worship, which are carried out in a particular way and have a special meaning.

Spelt A type of grain.

Symbolic Something that represents another. For example, the bitter herb represents the suffering of the Jewish slaves and so it is symbolic.

Synagogues Jewish community buildings for education, worship and social occasions.

Wilderness A desert.

BOOKS TO READ

I am a Jew by Clive Lawton (Watts, 1995)

Jewish Festivals by Angela Wood (Heinemann, 1996)

Judaism by Monica Stoppleman (Watts, 1996)

Judaism by Angela Wood (Wayland, 1995)

My Jewish Life by Anne Clarke (Wayland, 1996)

What Do We Know About Judaism? by Doreen Fine (Macdonald, 1996)

USEFUL ADDRESSES

To find out more about Judaism, you may find these addresses useful:

Board of Deputies of British Jews,
Commonwealth House,
1–19 New Oxford Street,
London, WC1A 1NF
Telephone 0171 543 5400

Jewish Music Distribution,
P.O. Box 2268,
Hendon, NW4 3UW
Telephone 0181 203 8046

Manor House Books,
Sternberg Centre,
80 East End Road,
Finchley, London, N3 2SY
Telephone 0181 346 2288

Memorial Council Bookshop,
25 Enford Street,
London, W1H 1DL
Telephone 0171 724 7778

INDEX